CHARLES B. & PATRICIA A.

TUBBS
CHILDREN'S
LIBRARY

Ecosystems

by Debra J. Housel

MISSION: SCIENCE

Science Contributor
Sally Ride Science
Science Consultants
Thomas R. Ciccone, Science Educator
Ronald Edwards, Science Educator

MISSION: SCIENCE

Developed with contributions from Sally Ride Science™

Sally Ride
Science

Sally Ride Science™ is an innovative content company dedicated to fueling young people's interests in science.

Our publications and programs provide opportunities for students and teachers to explore the captivating world of science—from astrobiology to zoology.

We bring science to life and show young people that science is creative, collaborative, fascinating, and fun.

To learn more, visit www.SallyRideScience.com

First hardcover edition published in 2009 by
Compass Point Books
151 Good Counsel Drive
P.O. Box 669
Mankato, MN 56002-0669

Editor: Mari Bolte
Designer: Heidi Thompson
Editorial Contributor: Sue Vander Hook

Art Director: LuAnn Ascheman-Adams
Creative Director: Joe Ewest
Editorial Director: Nick Healy
Managing Editor: Catherine Neitge

 This book was manufactured with paper containing at least 10 percent post-consumer waste.

Library of Congress Cataloging-in-Publication Data
Housel, Debra J.
  Ecosystems / by Debra J. Housel.
    p. cm. — (Mission: Science)
  Includes index.
  ISBN 978-0-7565-4068-5 (library binding)
  1. Biotic communities—Juvenile literature. I. Title. II. Series.
  QH541.14.H68 2009
  577—dc22   2008035730

Visit Compass Point Books on the Internet at *www.compasspointbooks.com*
or e-mail your request to *custserv@compasspointbooks.com*

Table of Contents

What Is an Ecosystem?

What kind of life could there be in the Mojave Desert? You might think animals can't exist in such a vast dry area of the western United States. But the jackrabbit can. Where rainfall is less than 10 inches (250 millimeters) per year, the jackrabbit survives. It adapts to temperatures that drop to well below freezing in the winter and soar above 130 degrees Fahrenheit (54 degrees Celsius) in the summer.

Every day the jackrabbit finds plants to eat. It eats sagebrush, mesquite, and even cactus. But it also has to watch out for coyotes and eagles—predators that eat jackrabbits.

There is a lot of life in the jackrabbit's world. All the living things in the Mojave Desert depend on one another to survive. The jackrabbit needs plants, and the coyotes need jackrabbits. Even the plants need the animals. Together, the plants and animals form an ecosystem—the plants and animals that need one another to survive in a particular environment.

The number of plants and animals must stay balanced in an ecosystem. Too many jackrabbits will eat the plants faster than they can grow back. And too many coyotes will run out of food before jackrabbits can reproduce.

Just one event can disturb the balance of an ecosystem. In the early 1900s, a group of Minnesota moose swam out to Isle Royale, an island in northern Lake Superior. They had no predators on the island, and within 10 years, there were 3,000 moose. But there weren't enough plants for all those moose to eat, so the moose started to die.

In 1949, a pair of wolves wandered across an ice bridge that spanned from Ontario, Canada, to Isle Royale. Now the moose had a predator, and their numbers decreased. Before long there were too many wolves, and many of them also starved. Scientists continue to study the changing balance among the moose, wolves, and plants on Isle Royale.

Isle Royale

wolves

moose

Did You Know?

Gray wolves were once the most common large predator in North America. But by the 1930s, only a few remained. They are listed as endangered in most parts of the United States.

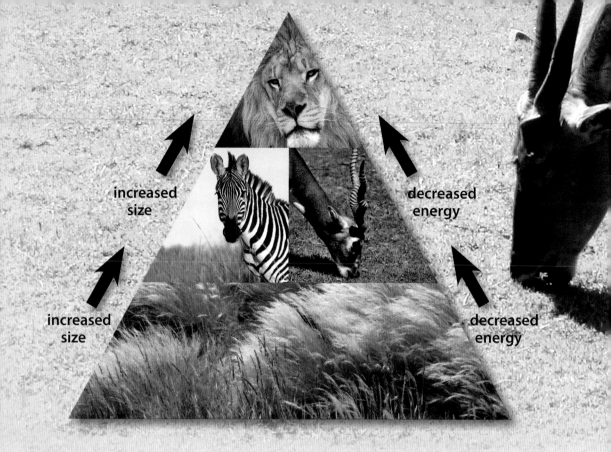

increased
size

decreased
energy

increased
size

decreased
energy

Every living thing in an ecosystem depends on another living thing for energy. This exchange of energy from one food source to another is part of an energy pyramid.

Plants are at the bottom of most energy pyramids. In fact, without plants, there would be no life on Earth. Green plants use light from the sun for photosynthesis, a chemical process by which plants make their own food. Plants also use nutrients from the soil.

Animals cannot make their own energy, so they must eat plants or other animals. They are called consumers because they eat other living things. When gazelles and zebras eat grass, they take energy and nutrients from the plants to run, eat, and mate. Later a lion may eat a gazelle or a zebra to get its own energy and nutrients. The gazelle and zebra had already used some of the energy from the grass, and the lion takes what is left. As you go up the energy pyramid

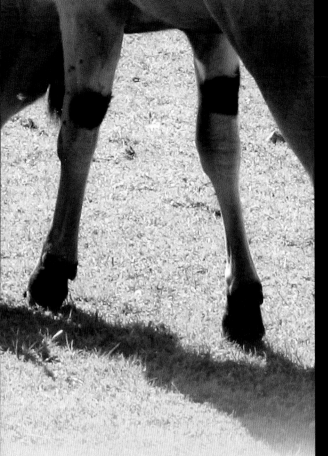

and the size of the consumer increases, the overall amount of energy transferred drops.

Eventually the lion dies. And decomposers such as worms, bacteria, and fungi break down the lion's remains. These decomposers use up some of the energy from the lion and return the rest of the nutrients to the soil. Now plants can use the nutrients in the soil, and a new energy pyramid begins.

Herbivores, Carnivores, and Omnivores

Animals are herbivores, carnivores, or omnivores. Herbivores eat only plants, while carnivores eat nothing but meat. Omnivores eat plants and animals. Giraffes are herbivores, able to nibble the highest branches of tall trees. Pandas are also herbivores, eating almost entirely low-lying bamboo.

Lions and tigers are carnivores, feasting on buffalo, zebras, giraffes, and more. Humans, on the other hand, are omnivores, with a diet of vegetables, fruits, grains, and meat. Other omnivores include bears, pigs, and crows.

Ecosystems can be quite complex. A carnivore may sometimes eat plants. And some herbivores, such as mice, ostriches, grasshoppers, and deer, do eat meat at times. In fact, in most ecosystems, organisms eat many different things.

Scientists have divided Earth into areas called biomes. Each biome has its own climate and vegetation. For example, a desert has dry weather and usually sand or rocks instead of soil. This affects the kinds of plants and animals that can live there.

Altitude and latitude determine biome boundaries. Altitude measures how high an area is above sea level. Latitude is the distance from the equator, the invisible line around the middle of Earth.

Altitude affects what can grow in a region. For example, trees only grow to a certain altitude. Where they stop growing is called the tree line. Above that, cold, wind, and lack of moisture prevent trees from growing. Most of the soil has also blown away, leaving just rocks where only short plants can grow. Sheep, elk, chinchillas, and birds survive there, getting their energy from low-lying vegetation.

Latitude helps determine how hot or cold a place may be. The closer it is to the equator, the hotter the weather. Farther away from the equator, temperatures drop. In the far north,

◄ The plant life and climate of an area can tell you something about its altitude and latitude.

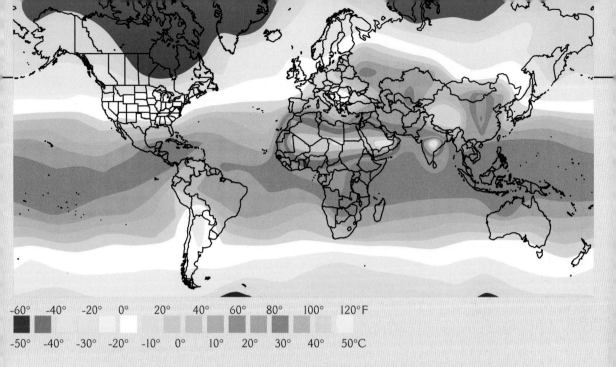

-60°	-40°	-20°	0°	20°	40°	60°	80°	100°	120°F
-50°	-40°	-30°	-20°	-10°	0°	10°	20°	30°	40°	50°C

▲ Various biomes, depicted as stripes, look as if they are stacked on top of each other. Warm biomes are close to the equator. Colder biomes are near the poles.

extremely low temperatures and short summers make it impossible for trees to grow. Only short grasses, lichens, and moss grow in these areas. In the summer, plants get their energy from the sun through photosynthesis during long spells of daylight. Caribou eat the grasses, and polar bears eat the caribou.

▲ Polar bears are the largest predators in the Arctic. They prevent the population of caribou from getting too big.

Land Biomes: Tundra

At the extreme northern part of Earth is a biome called the tundra. The temperatures in this biome are very low, and strong, frigid winds sweep across the land. The top layer of soil freezes in the winter and thaws in the summer. Below that is a layer called permafrost, which is soil that is frozen all year. The permafrost keeps water from draining deep into the ground, so the water forms ponds and bogs.

Trees don't grow in the tundra because their roots can't get past the permafrost. Instead, tundra regions grow grasses, lichens, and mosses, whose short roots are nourished in the top layer of soil. Animals that survive in the tundra include caribou, wolves, polar bears, snowy owls, and the mouselike vole.

Few people live in the tundra, but those who do need heat year-round. Heat used by humans can affect the biome's natural balance. When heat escapes from buildings, roads, and pipelines, it can thaw the permafrost. Global warming also melts the permafrost, creating more bogs than there would be naturally. During the past 100 years, the edge of permafrost has retreated about 50 miles (80.5 kilometers).

The snowy owl's thick, white plumage and feathered feet help it stay warm in the tundra. ➡

tundra

Caribou

Caribou are large deer that live in North America—they are also known as reindeer in other parts of the world. They travel in herds across the tundra, eating lichen and grasses. Sometimes they also eat birds and voles, which means they are omnivores. They travel in herds for protection from their predators, which are mainly wolves and polar bears. To stay warm in this cold biome, caribou have two layers of fur.

Tiny Tundra Dweller

The arctic ground squirrel spends most of its life asleep in a burrow just above the permafrost. While it sleeps, it lives off of its layer of fat. When the squirrel wakes up, it has 90 days to mate, raise its young, and eat enough food to build up a fat layer. To do this, it must work at least 17 hours a day. Then it curls up for another nine-month nap.

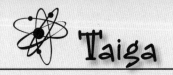
Just south of the tundra is the taiga, the largest land biome on Earth. The taiga covers much of Canada, Russia, and China. The taiga has only two seasons: winter and summer. Winters are long and cold, and summers are short and cool.

Evergreen trees, such as pine, spruce, and cedar, thrive in the cold, dry taiga. They grow well where there are fewer nutrients in the soil. These trees do not lose their leaves in the winter, which is the reason they are called evergreens.

Many animals live in the taiga, feeding on evergreens and other taiga vegetation. Birds build their nests in the trees, and deer hide in the shade of the branches. Grizzly bears, eagles, deer, and bats make their homes in these evergreen forests. This environment has many lakes, bogs, and rivers.

Did You Know?

Temperatures in the taiga are below freezing for half the year. Winter temperatures are usually between minus 65 F and 30 F (minus 54 C and minus 1 C).

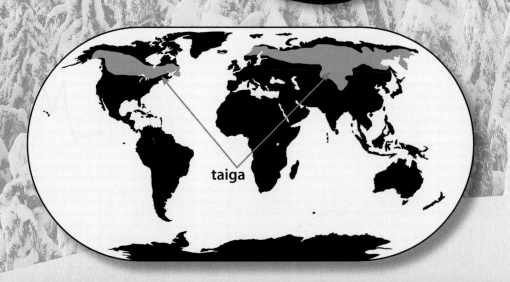

taiga

14

Protecting the Original Taiga

Most of Russia is a taiga biome. In fact, the word *taiga*, which means "cold forest," is Russian. Russia's vast northern land is home to arctic foxes, brown bears, musk deer, and snow leopards. But this unique region faces serious threats. Poachers hunt the animals illegally, and loggers break the law by cutting down trees. The climate is changing because of nearby cities. Russians don't want to lose their taiga. They have turned almost 10 million acres (4 million hectares) of taiga into protected land.

Black Bear

Black bears live in the taiga where they eat salmon, fawns, and rodents. They also eat berries, leaves, ants, and any other food they can find. Because it's so cold in the taiga, these large, strong creatures eat a variety of food to get energy and stay warm. Food adds layers of fat that help them stay warm. No other animal in the taiga hunts the enormous black bear. This makes the black bear an apex, or top-level, predator that is no other animal's prey. Apex predators appear at the top

Just south of the taiga, the weather warms up. Instead of two seasons, there are four: winter, spring, summer, and fall. This biome is called the temperate forest.

Evergreen trees are also found in the temperate forest, but there are many other trees and shrubs that are deciduous. Each fall, deciduous trees and plants lose their leaves. Deciduous means "tending to fall off." During the spring and summer, their leaves gather lots of sunlight. The trees store this energy and use it throughout the rest of the year. When the days get shorter and the nights get longer, deciduous trees and shrubs lose their leaves. Maple, beech, and oak trees are examples of deciduous trees.

Deer, raccoons, foxes, rabbits, and squirrels are just some of the animals that make their home in the temperate forest. Many people also live in this biome, where temperatures are pleasant most of the year. But people often alter the natural balance of a biome. In the temperate forest, people have cut down many of the trees to make room for their homes, farms, and orchards. Now people all over the world are replanting trees to replace the diminishing forests.

Peregrine Falcon

The peregrine falcon lives in the temperate forest. It is the fastest animal on the planet, soaring high into the air and then diving toward the ground at speeds up to 185 miles (300 km) per hour. This rapid plunge is called a stoop. When hunting other birds, the falcon uses the stoop to snatch its prey right out of the air. Peregrine falcons hunt doves and ducks in the wilderness. Some falcons have moved into big cities, making their nests on top of skyscrapers and hunting pigeons.

Working Together to Save the Pandas

The giant panda, found only in the temperate forests of China, needs a special kind of forest—a bamboo forest—to survive. But many bamboo forests have been cut down. At first China made it illegal to cut down the forest or hunt the animals in the ecosystem. But the local people needed food to eat and wood to burn for heat. So they broke the laws and broke into the reserves.

Now China is working to find ways for local people to help preserve the ecosystem. Locals are allowed to have farms, but they are changing their practices to keep the forests healthier. Instead of wood, they are burning biogas (gas made from the decay of living matter) in their stoves. Every effort, no matter how small, will help protect the forests and save the pandas.

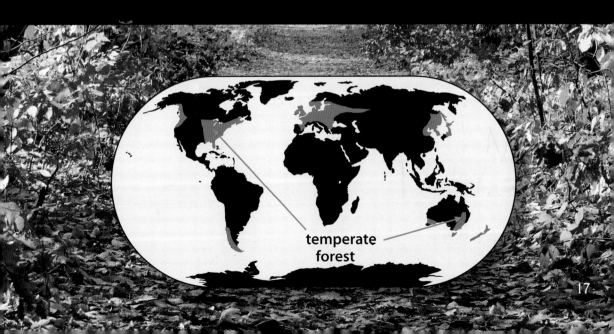

temperate forest

Tropical Rain Forest

Near the equator, the climate is warm. Temperatures don't vary much, averaging about 80 F (26 C) year-round. The biome at this latitude is the tropical rain forest. It rains almost constantly in this area of thick vegetation. The Amazon rain forest in South America is the world's largest. Others are in Central America, Asia, Africa, and Australia.

Tropical rain forests are home to millions of types of plants and animals. These forests cover less than 7 percent of Earth's land, yet about two-thirds of the world's plant and animal species live here. The plant life in this biome soaks up carbon dioxide. Since this is one of the gases that cause global warming, tropical rain forests help to reduce this problem.

At the top of a rain forest is a canopy of tree branches that overlap each other. Little sunlight gets through this dense foliage. Very few plants can grow on the forest floor, where very little sunlight peaks through. Many of these plants have dark red leaves, which helps them use the little light that reaches them. Other plants on the forest floor trap and eat bugs, which are in abundant supply.

People have destroyed a lot of the rain forests. They have cut down trees for logging, mining, and construction. They have built roads, houses, farms, and oil wells. In the past 30 years, about 20 percent of all the rain forests have been cut down and cleared for human habitation. Scientists think that dozens of rain forest species become extinct daily.

The Comeback of the Hyacinth Macaw

The beautiful blue hyacinth macaw almost became extinct. It was so pretty that it became a very popular pet for humans. Thousands of hyacinth macaws were captured in the South American rain forest in Brazil. They were sold illegally for a very high price.

At the same time, Brazilian farmers were cutting down trees in the rain forest to plant fields. These trees had been nesting places for many macaws. In time, there were only about 2,000 hyacinth macaws left in the world. A group of Brazilians decided it was time to save the hyacinth macaw from extinction. They nailed boxes to the tops of telephone poles. The birds were fooled. They thought the poles were trees and made their nests inside the boxes. The farmers were also persuaded to leave some trees standing so the birds would have a place to nest. Brazilian farmers are now proud to have hyacinth macaws on their farms.

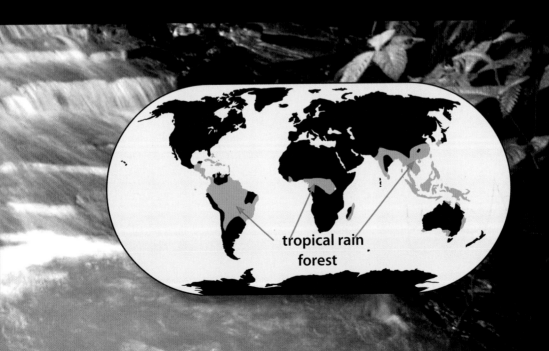

tropical rain forest

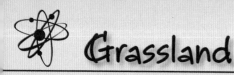
The grassland is a biome found in areas with hot, dry summers and mild, wet winters. Grassland biomes are in parts of the United States, Mexico, and Chile, and in much of Australia and South Africa. Grasslands cover one-fourth of Earth's land and are on every continent except Antarctica.

In Africa, zebras and giraffes graze on the grasslands. Large numbers of buffalo once made the grasslands of the North American plains their home. Now sheep and cattle have nearly replaced them. Natural grasslands are home to evergreen bushes that never grow more than 10 feet (3 meters) tall. In some places, these shrubs grow so close together that it's hard to pass through the area.

Hot Chili for Elephants

In Namibia, Africa, farmers had a problem with elephants. The huge, hungry creatures would crash through fences to get at the crops in their fields. The farmers built stronger fences, put up barbed wire, and rang bells to scare the elephants off. But nothing stopped them. The farmers had to think of a better way.

Then someone put up a fence made of ropes tied to poles. The farmers laughed. That wouldn't stop an elephant! But the elephants didn't crash through the ropes, and they stayed away. The farmers wanted to know why. The ropes had been dipped in hot chilis, and the elephants didn't like the smell. Now all the farmers grow a little patch of chilis next to their fences to keep elephants away.

It doesn't rain often in grasslands. When storms do come, lightning often strikes the dry grass and starts raging wildfires that can spread for hundreds of miles. Grassland plants depend on the fires to keep balance in the biome. Fires clear the brush and release essential minerals back into the soil. After a fire, seeds quickly sprout, and new grass begins to grow.

Many of the world's farms and ranches are found in the grasslands, where grains provide food for cattle.

Keep Your Eyes Peeled

The meadow argus butterfly lives in the outback of Australia. Like other butterflies, it eats nectar from flowers and keeps an eye out for birds and other predators. Fortunately the meadow argus has a defense mechanism that fools its enemies. On its wings are black spots that look like eyes. The butterfly appears large and dangerous. If the enemy is fooled, it will look for safer prey. Predators are often fooled into attacking the wing instead of the body, which saves the butterfly's life.

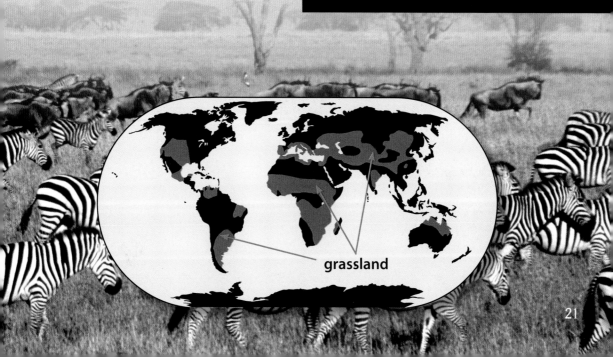

grassland

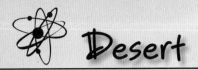

Desert

Some places on Earth hardly ever get rain. Mountains block the winds that bring rain clouds, and the land remains dry. This biome is called a desert. Most deserts are very hot. During the day, the sun scorches the land, and temperatures sometimes reach 122 F (50 C) in the shade. At night, temperatures can drop near freezing.

Desert plants have adapted to these harsh conditions. Some have very long water-seeking roots. Others, such as the cactus, store water in their stems and roots. Their sharp needles keep animals from getting too much of this water. To avoid the heat, most desert animals sleep during the day. At night, they come out and look for food. Some desert animals such as camels can store water in their bodies. Others, like burrowing

Meerkats

Meerkats are small rodents that live in Africa's Kalahari Desert. Every day they have to find food on the dry land. They dig up insects, steal eggs, and eat scorpions—stingers and all. Meerkats are small, but they can do mighty things when they work together. They go out to find food in groups—called a mob or a gang. One meerkat watches for hawks. When it spots one, it barks, and all of them hide until the barking stops. One or two meerkats stay behind to baby-sit the mob's young. Meerkats are also very playful. They often wrestle and race one another around their burrow. But even while they're playing, at least one meerkat watches out for predators.

desert

owls, get liquid from the animals they eat. The thorny devil, an Australian lizard, sits outside and lets dew collect on its spiny body. Its skin has many spines and grooves, which channel the moisture to its mouth.

Continent	Largest Deserts
Africa	Sahara (largest on Earth), Libyan, Namib, Kalahari
Asia	Arabian, Rub'al Khali, Gobi, Kara-Kum, Kyzyl-Kum, Takla Makan, Kavir, Syrian, Thar, Dasht-e-Lut
Australia	Great Victoria, Great Sandy, Gibson, Simpson
North America	Great Basin, Chihuahuan, Sonoran, Colorado, Yuma, Mojave
South America	Patagonian, Atacama
Antarctica	Entire continent

Water Biomes: Freshwater

Probably the most important of all the biomes are the water biomes: freshwater and marine saltwater. Since people and land animals cannot drink seawater, which is salty, they depend on the world's freshwater supply. Earth is covered mostly by water, but only 3 percent of its water is fresh. And most of that is trapped in polar ice.

The freshwater biomes are very precious because they have running fresh water. Rivers, lakes, and estuaries support fish, ducks, frogs, and turtles, as well as cattails and water plants. Wetlands, with their bogs and marshes of standing water, are important because they store water and stop floods. Some plants and animals, such as salamanders and alligators, can live only in wetlands. Certain plants and trees, such as the cypress, grow well in standing water or slow-moving water in swamps.

People have altered some of the freshwater biomes by draining the water or filling in wetlands with dirt. Wetlands are replaced with homes, farms, and businesses.

New York is Cleaning Up Its Act

New York City lies along the banks of the Hudson River. The river was the reason people built the city there in the first place. Over time, some large electric and manufacturing companies on the banks of the river polluted the water with chemicals.

Fish and wildlife were contaminated, which also posed a health risk to humans. Some people wanted the river cleaned up. In 2006, a plan was approved to remove the harmful chemicals from the bottom of the river. The U.S. Environmental Protection Agency began working with area factories to begin the cleanup process and remove the chemicals.

These biomes are also affected when fertilizer runs off lawns and farms and collects in lakes or ponds. Added nutrients from the fertilizer cause algae such as seaweed to grow rapidly, or bloom. The additional growth blocks sunlight from reaching deep into the water. Algae blooms can also lower oxygen levels in the water. Without enough sunlight and oxygen, fish will die.

Mosquito Menace

Mosquitoes breed out of control when wetlands are drained. How can this be when mosquitoes thrive in wetlands? Mosquitoes will keep breeding in rain puddles and leftover ponds. Without wetlands, there are no homes for the predators that eat mosquitoes. When a 1,500-acre (600-hectare) wetland was restored, mosquitoes decreased by 90 percent.

Marine Biomes

Salt water covers almost 75 percent of Earth. Oceans, seas, and coral reefs are all marine biomes. These biomes support life of all shapes and sizes, from microscopic plants and animals to the blue whale, the largest animal on Earth. Marine algae supply much of the world's oxygen and absorb huge amounts of carbon dioxide.

Coral reefs are colorful biomes produced by living organisms in warm, shallow parts of the ocean. Coral reefs can be found up to 30 degrees north and south latitude of the equator. One out of four ocean species makes its home on coral reefs. But coral reefs are sensitive to temperature. Global warming has heated the seawater, causing an imbalance on the coral reefs. If the water doesn't cool down, coral reefs could die within 50 years.

Did You Know?

Australia's Great Barrier Reef is the largest reef in the world. It is more than 1,400 miles (2,300 km) long and is home to more than 1,500 species of fish and 400 species of coral. Scientists consider it to be the largest living organism in the world.

Coral Reefs

A piece of coral may look like a strange rock, but it's actually a whole colony of animals. The hard, rocklike part is a protective shell that grows around microscopic animals called polyps. It takes millions of polyps to make a coral reef. Coral needs its water to be just right. If the water heats up too much, the coral turns white and dies. This is called coral bleaching. The bleached part of a coral reef can never recover. The Great Barrier Reef of Australia recently had its worst coral bleaching

Turtle Tours

On a special beach near Tortuguero ("Region of Turtles"), Costa Rica, green turtles come out of the ocean to dig nests, lay their eggs, and cover them with sand. Then the turtles return to the sea. Between 45 and 75 days later, baby turtles hatch and instinctively head directly into the ocean. Predators such as seagulls and crabs eat many of them before they reach the water.

The people of Tortuguero fed their families by hunting the turtles and harvesting their eggs. They also exported the turtles, which were popular for turtle soup. The people were very good at this—too good, in fact. Every year, there were fewer turtles.

When the animal nearly became extinct, the people of Tortuguero formed an agency to study and protect the turtles. They stopped hunting the turtles and stopped harvesting their eggs. In 1970, the area became a national park where people from all over the world come to see the turtles. Tourists have helped the economy, and the residents run hotels, tours, and restaurants. Touring fragile ecosystems instead of hunting and harvesting is called ecotourism.

You and Your Ecosystem

The natural ecosystems and biomes in the world live with a vast variety of climates, vegetation, and animal life. Humans inhabit nearly all of them. People like you are part of the natural world, and you are part of the ecosystem in which you live. Each ecosystem depends on a delicate balance that keeps all the living organisms in it alive.

Imbalance threatens ecosystems all over the world. Disrupting the natural environment of any ecosystem can lead to extinction of plants and animals. When a species is in danger of dying out, it is considered an endangered species.

Humans must protect the ecosystems of the world, being careful not to harm their delicate balances. Careless city expansion, polluting, hunting, or rearrangement of the land can harm our ecosystems. A safe and healthy future depends on thriving biomes. We must do all we can to preserve and protect them. We can start by conserving water, recycling, and reducing pollution.

Things You Can Do

- Reduce the amount of trash you throw away.

- Reuse paper, jars, and boxes instead of throwing them away.

- Recycle plastic, aluminum, glass, and paper.

- Clean up local wetlands, parks, or wilderness areas.

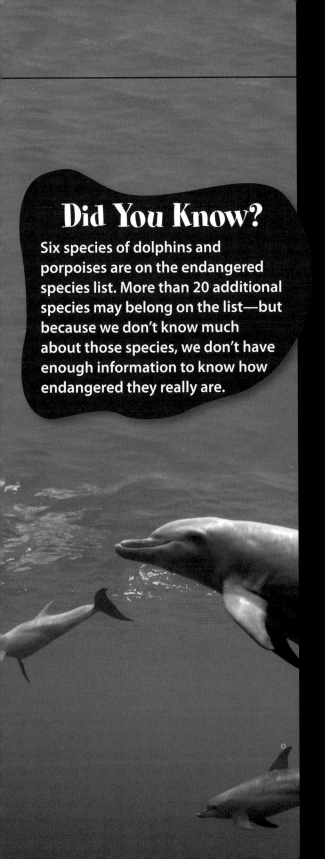

Did You Know?

Six species of dolphins and porpoises are on the endangered species list. More than 20 additional species may belong on the list—but because we don't know much about those species, we don't have enough information to know how endangered they really are.

Danger for Dolphins

The Bosporus Strait through the country of Turkey is the world's narrowest international passageway. This 20-mile (32-km) stretch is also one of the busiest shipping routes in the world. On both sides of the strait lies the bustling city of Istanbul. Fishing boats, ferries, freighters, and oil tankers make their way through the channel every day.

The Bosporus Strait is also home to many dolphins. They use the strait to migrate back and forth between the Black Sea and the Sea of Marmara, which connects to the Aegean Sea and then to the Mediterranean Sea. It is a dangerous place for dolphins, which must constantly dodge the huge vessels in the swift current. They stay in small groups, aware of the danger around them.

Some marine biologists think the dolphins should be protected. Once a week they survey the strait by boat, checking on how the dolphins are doing. The biologists study where they live and what they eat. They hope to use this information to convince the Turkish government to protect the dolphins' territory.

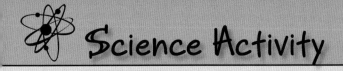
Create an Algae Bloom

With a few materials, you can create your own algae bloom. In this activity, you will observe pond plants growing in normal pond water. You will also observe pond plants growing in water with fertilizer added. The fertilizer is the same substance people use to make their lawns more beautiful or help plants grow better on farms. After two weeks, you will compare the growth of the plants as well as the condition of the water.

Materials

- fresh water from a pond or lake (you can use tap water, but it will slow down the activity)

- two clean, clear glass jars with screw-type metal lids; a 16-ounce (480-milliliter) jar is ideal

- liquid lawn fertilizer

- floating water plants (one tablespoon (15 mL) of algae from a pond works best)

- ¼ teaspoon measure

- masking tape

- pen

Procedure

1 Fill the two glass jars with pond or lake water.

2 Place a floating water plant or some algae in each jar.

3 Use the masking tape and pen to label one jar "Pond Water" and the other jar "Fertilized Water."

4 Place ¼ teaspoon of liquid lawn fertilizer in the jar labeled Fertilized Water. Stir it thoroughly with the measuring spoon. Screw on the jar's lid.

5 Place both jars in the sunlight.

6 Observe the jars daily and record the changes you observe in each jar. Include changes in the water as well as the plants or algae.

7 After one week, place another ¼ teaspoon of liquid lawn fertilizer in the Fertilized Water jar.

8 Observe the jars daily for another week and record your observations.

9 Write down your final conclusions about each jar at the end of the second week.

Conclusion

You will see that the pond plants in the Pond Water jar are growing at a normal pace. The water beneath the plants is relatively clear. The pond plants in the Fertilized Water jar are growing rapidly and taking up all the space. The water below them is cloudy and murky. If there were fish in that jar, they would die because of the plant overgrowth.

Rachel Carson (1907–1964)
American marine biologist and ecologist whose writings brought attention to environmental concerns and helped spread the environmental movement

Aldo Leopold (1887–1948)
American ecologist who roused public interest in wildlife conservation and encouraged the development of game preserves and national forests; wrote *A Sand County Almanac*

Jane Lubchenco (1947–   )
American environmentalist who brought the problem of global warming to the public's attention; discovered dead zones in lakes where no fish live; helped make the environment an important political issue

Neo Martinez (1958–   )
University professor who created a computer model in a special lab to illustrate food webs and explain the intricate links among plants and animals in an ecosystem

Eugene Odum (1913–2002)
American scientist who studied ecosystems, determining how animals, plants, and climate interconnect to balance the ecosystem; worked with Ruth Patrick to gather data on water quality and living organisms in the Savannah River

Ruth Patrick (1907–   )
Freshwater specialist who studied freshwater ecosystems and invented the diatometer to measure and determine the impact of pollution in fresh water

Charles Sutherland Elton (1900–1991)
British ecologist who developed the idea that living things form a pyramid of food levels that keep the energy flow within an ecosystem in balance; at the base are producers, and at the top are consumers

John Woodward (1665–1728)
English naturalist who discovered that plants in dirty water grew faster than plants in pure water

33

Glossary

altitude—height of some-thing above sea level or Earth's surface

apex predator—predator at the top of its food chain; not preyed upon by others

biome—large area that shares the same general climate of temperature and rainfall

bogs—areas of wet and spongy ground

canopy—uppermost layer in the rain forest, formed by the crown of the trees

carnivore—animal that eats only meat

climate—conditions in the atmosphere in a particular place over periods of time

consumer—animal that eats

deciduous—plants and trees that shed or lose their leaves

decomposers—organisms, usually bacteria or fungi, that break down dead plants and animals into simpler substances

desert—dry, often sandy region with little rainfall, extreme temperatures, and sparse vegetation

ecosystem—interaction between a community of plants and animals living in a natural environment

ecotourism—tourism to exotic or threatened ecosystems to observe wildlife or to help preserve nature

endangered—plant or animal with such few numbers that it may become extinct

equator—imaginary line that goes around the middle of Earth halfway between the North and South Poles

evergreen—plant, tree, or bush that keeps its leaves throughout the year

extinct—plant or animal that has died out; there will never be any more like it

fertilizers—substances, such as manure or chemicals, to make soil richer and better for growing crops

global warming—rise in the average worldwide temperature

grassland—land where grass or grasslike vegetation grows; found in areas with hot, dry summers and mild, wet winters

herbivore—animal that eats only plants

latitude—position of a place measured in degrees north or south of the equator

nutrients—substances, such as vitamins, that plants and animals need for good health

omnivore—animal that eats both plants and animals

permafrost—ground that is permanently frozen

photosynthesis—process by which plants make food using sunlight, carbon dioxide, and water

predator—animal that hunts and eats other animals; for example, a toad is a bug's predator

rain forest—forest with heavy annual rainfall

taiga—largest biome on Earth; its pine forests border the tundra

temperate forest—forest in regions with moderate temperatures

tundra—large, treeless areas of northern Asia, North America, and Europe where the subsoil is permanently frozen

100	Chinese invent the first insecticide using a powder of dried chrysanthemum flowers
1804	Nicholas de Saussure discovers that plants need carbon dioxide from the air and nitrogen from the soil
1898	The Rivers and Harbors Act bans pollution of navigable waters in the United States
1908	Chlorination is first used to treat water, making the water 10 times purer than when filtered
1916	The U.S. National Park Service is established
1934	Russian ecologist G.F. Gause determines that two similar species cannot occupy the same ecosystem for long periods of time; called Gause's principle
1935	U.S. Soil Conservation Service is established
1956	Water Pollution Control Act makes federal money available for water treatment plants
1962	Rachel Carson publishes Silent Spring, a look at the dangers of the unchecked use of pesticides in nature
1970	National Environmental Policy Act is established, calling for federal agencies to issue an environmental impact statement for all construction projects
1972	DDT, a pesticide that caused a decline in several bird species, is phased out in the United States
1976	Studies show that the chlorofluorocarbons from spray cans contribute to the decrease in the ozone

1978	Residents are evacuated from Love Canal, New York, after discovering a major chemical waste dump
1979	Three Mile Island nuclear power plant in Pennsylvania experiences a near meltdown
1987	The Montreal Protocol is signed by 24 countries, reducing and eventually phasing out the use of chlorofluorocarbons by the end of the century
1988	Radon contamination found to be more prevalent in U.S. homes than previously thought
1990	Scientists determine that 1990 is the warmest year on record
1991	The United States agrees to protect Antarctica from mineral excavation and to preserve the region's native flora and fauna
1992	Small amounts of ozone depletion are reported for the first time in the Northern Hemisphere
1993	The ozone hole over Antarctica reaches record size, thought to be the continuing result of the volcanic eruption of Mount Pinatubo in the Philippines
2005	The Kyoto Protocol takes effect; most countries agree to restrict their greenhouse gas emissions by set amounts; the United States refuses to sign the agreement
2008	Scientists find that nitrogen pollution is causing harm to marine ecosystems and contributing to global warming

Jackson, Tom. *Tropical Forests*. Austin, Texas: Raintree Publishers, 2003.

Nardo, Don. *Climate Crisis: The Science of Global Warming*. Minneapolis: Compass Point Books, 2008.

Steele, Christy. *Grassland Animals*. Austin, Texas: Raintree Steck-Vaughn Publishers, 2002.

Stille, Darlene. *The Greenhouse Effect: Warming the Planet*. Minneapolis: Compass Point Books, 2006.

Stille, Darlene. *Nature Interrupted: The Science of Environmental Chain Reactions*. Minneapolis: Compass Point Books, 2008.

On the Web

For more information on this topic, use FactHound.
1. Go to *www.facthound.com*
2. Choose your grade level.
3. Begin your search.
This book's ID number is 9780756540685
FactHound will find the best sites for you.

Index

Debra J. Housel

Debra Housel earned a master's degree from Nazareth College of Rochester and worked as a teacher for more than a dozen years before becoming a freelance writer. She has written more than 80 titles for the education market, some of them award-winning. Debra is an avid environmentalist, and she appreciates the beauties of the natural world. She lives in Rochester, New York, where she enjoys being outdoors and observing the world around her.

Image Credits